COOCH
MR CHILCOTT TO YOU

COOCH
MR CHILCOTT TO YOU

The experiences of Gareth Chilcott

by
GARETH CHILCOTT
with Tony Ferrand

JOHNSONS PUBLISHING LTD

Published by Johnsons Publishing Ltd
Grayson House
12–16 Clerkenwell Road
London EC1M 5PQ

ISBN 1 873304 00 5

Cover designed by The Headline Group, Headline House,
3 & 4 Riverside Court, Lower Bristol Road, Bath, Avon BA2 3DZ

Cover photography by Jonathan Metcalf

Photoset by Avon Phototypesetting Limited
Printed in Great Britain by
Redwood Press Limited
Bowerhill, Melksham, Wiltshire.
Binding by Bath Press Ltd
Lower Bristol Road, Bath, Avon

Cartoons by Paul Davies

FOREWORD

I had heard many stories pertaining to a certain Gareth Chilcott, when I was a keen young prop with Exeter University. I'll be honest and say not many of them gave the impression that he was seeking to become a 'freeman' of the city of Bath, in fact I had the distinct impression that he was likely to become a very unfree man with Her Majesty's Prison Service before too long.

It was therefore an enormous surprise when I met 'Cooch' shortly after joining Bath Football Club (RFU) in 1983. He was the personification of charm itself. As the months passed and I spent more time with him, it became apparent that he was one of the most honest, honourable and reliable people I had ever met.

As a prop, loosehead or tighthead, he has had few peers in recent years. If I was playing for Bath 1st XV and Cooch was being 'rested' in the 2nd XV, training sessions leading up to the respective fixtures were always hard, particularly the scrummaging when Cooch and I were in direct contact. To say that I spent that half hour in extreme discomfort is an understatement, I just hope he felt some discomfort in return.

Having played with him on numerous occasions, I have the utmost respect for him, for on the field he was uncompromising, hard and ruthless – and at the same time courageous, taking beatings without a murmur, yet ensuring that he was never beaten! While off the field, he was intent on pursuing the social aspects of rugby with equal zeal!

If it's a charity event or helping a mate, Cooch is always the first to volunteer his services. I am sure that this attitude to life causes some friction at home due to the amount of time he does spend 'helping people out'. His wife Ann has my sympathy, but this commitment off the field has won him many friends the world over, friendships that will last for many years when his playing days are over.

I have heard the phrase 'Poacher turned Gamekeeper' used as a description of Gareth. I would not use as many words, I would just describe him as a Gentleman.

Finally I wish him all the very best with this book and in the future – in the meantime, have an enjoyable read.

David Sole
Captain of Scotland (RFU)
September 1990

To my wife Ann

also
To all the people who
have helped me through the
harder times, you know
who you are.

CONTENTS

EARLY YEARS

NEWTS have always figured in my life. At school I spent the biology lessons combing the local ponds for newts and weeds for the bright kids to learn about in the next lesson. Having escaped from Ashton Park Comprehensive school, my post rugby activity was likened to that of a newt.

Some people are academic, I'm an acadon't. I was at my happiest pursuing a ball, round or oval shaped it made no difference. Cricket, soccer or rugby were my life. It may shock rugby purists to know that I was once a card carrying supporter of Bristol City Football Club.

I followed the reds for years and, I fear, I was not always their most meek and mild supporter. I was invited to a dinner at Ashton Gate and, after I had been introduced to the directors and their bar, was invited to say a few words: "Well," I recalled with the inspiration that Courage Best offers a speaker faced with an eager and receptive audience, "About 18 years ago I heaved a brick through that window there and a year later I heaved one through this window here." They didn't seem to mind too much, in fact most of them had a little chuckle. With hindsight: they probably didn't believe me. Anyway the idea broke the ice as well as the window and they have yet to send me the bill for the glazing.

Sport was the only subject at school in which I showed any promise and I left at 15 with nothing in the way of

ASHTON GATE
BRISTOL CITY
FOOTBALL CLUB

UNDER THIS
WINDOW
GARETH CHILCOTT
LEARNT HOW TO
PUT THE BALL
INTO A LINEOUT..
..UNFORTUNATELY
HE USED
A BRICK!

qualifications and precious little ambition. Some eight months on the dole later I was finding getting regular work a bit of a problem. There didn't seem to be too many employers looking for a totally unqualified tearaway to join their payroll. It was a teacher to whom I had given a fairly hard time at Ashton Park who pushed me into joining the Old Redcliffians, a strong Bristol Combination club. Had it not been for Norman Ridgeway who pushed me towards the Old Reds I would probably not have gone on to success in both rugby and business.

Because they are south of the river Avon, the Reds count as a Somerset side and have made something of a habit of winning the Somerset Cup. They were a side that played hard and knew how to celebrate after the game. I found rugby with the Old Reds a good way of letting off steam and also liked having a few beers and a sing song with the lads after the game. There's nothing as satisfying as a good maul in the mud, eight pints of Best and Four and Twenty Virgins for afters.

...DO YOU HAVE ANY VACANCIES FOR A FULLY QUALIFIED TEARAWAY WHO KNOWS EVERY VERSE OF 'ERE WE GO ERE WE GO ERE WE GO!?

The first season I hooked for the Under 18 side but then moved to tight head prop, generally reckoned to be the easier of the two sides because the player has both shoulders in contact with the opposition while the loose head has only one. Most people can only play on one side, among them the Scotland skipper, David Sole who played so well for Bath until he went back up North. Due to circumstances that have arisen over the years, I have had sufficient practice to enable me to play both loose and tight.

I did well enough at the Old Reds to listen to suggestions that I might try my luck with a senior club. It is not generally known that I went up to Bristol for a training session prior to the 1975-6 season. I didn't enjoy it at all. There was no sense of being on the same side. Afterwards the first team men were in one group and the United players in another. With us glaring at the first teamers and the unspoken message: "Bastards! We want your places."

The first team were far too grand to demean themselves to speak to the United players and I as a new boy was beneath

EVERYBODY'S notice. Nobody spoke to us new boys at all. So off I went to Bath where everybody mixed in together, first fifteen, United, Spartans, it was all much friendlier and I think the team worked together better as a result.

Even so I still had problems which were not Bath's fault. At Old Reds everyone seemed to come from the same sort of social background. But at Bath there were people like Charlie Ralston, a doctor and Jim Waterman, a headmaster. I didn't know quite how to approach them. I did well as a player, getting straight into the United side and, after eight games with them, being promoted to the Firsts where I held my place.

Although I was accepted as a player, I didn't know how to mix socially with them so after each game I would shoot off and join my mates from the Old Reds for a few beers, getting drunk with them was relaxing, we spoke the same language.

The older Bath players still laugh about what I was like then. I would turn up, change, charge around the field doing as much damage as possible - at that time I had very little

technique but made up for it with any amount of natural aggression - then after the game I would shower and change, pull on my woolly Bristol City hat and dash off without saying a word to anyone. I did that for about three years, too! It wasn't that the Bath players weren't friendly, I just didn't feel at home with professional people like that.

My third game for Bath was to be a certain defeat at the hands of Swansea at St Helens. At the time Swansea were exceptionally strong and we didn't have the forwards to sort out a top line English club let alone the best the Welsh could throw at us.

We duly took our hammering, one player in particular found himself typecast as a punchbag. Poor Brian Jenkins was nearly driven into the ground like a tentpeg by his opposite number and all because he had a nervous tic. The Welsh front jumper, Geoff Wheel, also had a nervous tic that would jerk his head around. This became most obvious when waiting for the ball in the lineout when a combination of the tension of waiting to jump for the ball and the stillness

of the players had Geoff's head twitching away like a mechanical toy.

Unfortunately for Brian he suffered from the same thing and the sight of the pair of them ticking away at the head of the lineout was like something out of a comedy film. Geoff did not know that Brian had the same problem and was convinced that he was taking the Mickey. Eventually this apparent taunting was too much for Geoff who thumped his opponent around the ear. This was not very nice for poor Brian, Geoff being 17 $^{1}/_{2}$ stone and built like the proverbial brick outhouse with the strength of ten. Being struck with a fist like a JCB shovel apparently does not cure a twitch. In fact it seems to make it worse. The more Geoff clobbered Brian the more his singing head twitched.

We were all glad when the game was over but none so much as Brian who was fearing permanent brain damage at the hand of the Welsh piledriver. It was only in the bar after the game that Geoff discovered his opposite number had the

same affliction. He was mortified. Apologies flowed as did the beer and Brian did not need to put his hand in his pocket all night.

I suppose this running punch-up illustrates rather well how hard it is for the referee to spot minor battles taking place away from the ball. The ball is the hub of the game. It has to be put into the scrum straight and thrown straight into the lineout, it is one of the keys to offside decisions, it must be passed backwards and mustn't be knocked forwards.

So it is, that the referee must have his eye on the ball at all times. Small wonder that fist fights twenty or thirty yards away from the vital ball all too often go unnoticed. Touch judges have the power to intervene in international matches, perhaps it would be a good idea to extend this to club games. In my early days with Bath I quite enjoyed a spot of gratuitous violence on the side, it added something to the game, spice perhaps, spice of life.

BLUE BLACK WHITE - AND GREEN

JOINING Bath was probably one of the most sensible moves I have made in my life and yet it was a strange one for an 18 year old from Bedminster. There's me recently escaped from school, having carefully avoided any form of academic distinction, joining a side whose members included a public school master, a doctor, an orthopaedic surgeon, a solicitor and lord knows what other professions.

To begin with I was worried that I could not communicate with these rather superior beings. After training or a match, as I have already said, I would not go back to the club house, I would leg it back to Bristol and go for a drink with my mates in the Old Reds.

At that time Mike Fry, arguably the hardest man in English rugby, took me under his wing. He would take me round the Bedminster pubs where I was introduced as "my puppy". This puppy had a lot in common with Mike.

He was not very big for a prop. But what he lacked in size he well made up for in aggression and pride. Where weight could not succeed, he used strength and determination. Quite happy to hand out violence, he was not one to complain when it was returned.

"I live by the sword ... " he would say and he was never what he would call "babbie assed", that is to say he never complained to the press or anyone else when on the receiving end of a pre-emptive piece of gratuitous violence. But here was a man who survived in a very tough world with the aid of true skill as well as attack.

This skill was what I lacked and I learned a great deal from a man who was at the end of his career as I was at the start of mine. A few years later when I was pack leader of Somerset, they dropped me for a time for being too aggressive, which would have made total sense had they not replaced me as prop and vice captain with the Greek (Mike Fry), who was every bit as rough as me.

Bath was a strange club when I first joined it. Not only were there people from a completely different planet playing for the side but it was strangely inconsistent. One match we'd win by 40 points and the next we'd lose by the same margin. It was a top class club but it was capable of being beaten by sides of much lower standing in the rugby world.

Two things happened to weld me into the side. Jim Waterman, a great captain, instituted training on Mondays that was followed by a visit to a Bath pub that was a bit like the Windmill - we never close. When you have watched a doctor staggering around the bar almost blowing bubbles at four in the morning you cannot feel inhibited by the guy.

I had one distinct advantage over my team mates at the time, I was on the dole and didn't have to try and get up for work in the mornings. I believe you have to sign a statement to the effect that you are ready and available for work when you sign on. On Tuesday mornings the average knackers yard would have turned me down as unfit for petfood let alone work.

The other great influence in bringing us together as a real team was the tours. Thanks to rugby there's hardly a country in the world I haven't visited. In those early days it was not exactly like travelling with the England team. No five star hotels for us then. You tended to stay as a guest of your opposite number in the foreign team.

Not all of them were that well off for spare beds. A mattress on the floor in Montreal may have sounded primitive but it was better than the back of a van in a garage in Amsterdam. The club obviously has a certain amount of money to help

send you abroad and when you are away you never have to put your hand in your pocket for a beer.

One of the first tours I went on with Bath took us to Canada where we were guests of a club in Pentikton and our first day was a free one. They took us to a lakeside centre where we could spend the entire day on the sport of our choice. Water skiing, jet ski, wind surfing, sailing, riding, shooting ... anything you wanted to do was yours, and free at that.

To be honest I wasn't in a terribly energetic mood and did not fancy an activity packed day. I preferred the idea of soaking up a bit of the local culture, so, in the company of John Horton, a master at Kingswood public school in Bath and David Trick who was reading law at Bath University, we investigated the intellectual delicacies of Slack Alice's, the local strip joint.

This was a 24-hour programme of genteel and artistic striptease, thus it was 14 hours after entering Slack Alice's we were on first name terms with the barman and knew the anatomy of the four resident strippers every bit as well as their husbands. After this cultural experience together, John, Tricky and I became the greatest of mates.

I also became rather more part of the team and gradually we began to build up from being an erratic side, that had bursts of brilliance and moments of insane failure, into something rather more reliable. The real turning point for Bath came with the appointment of Roger Spurrell as captain.

We worked together rather well. He'd start the trouble and I'd finish it. An ideal partnership really. He was a Cornishman and a shepherd with some brilliant ideas for honing us particular sheep into something with a truly hard edge.

In the late seventies the Welsh teams were the hardest and the best. There was hardly an English club that would voluntarily take on a Welsh side. They knew they would be thrashed in every sense of the word. We had the advantage of being quite close to the bridge and Roger deliberately sought matches with the Welsh clubs.

This baptism of fire began with my third match with Bath when we were duly lined up for a ritual defeat at the hands

of Swansea. They were one of the best of the Welsh sides at the time. I was goggle eyed playing against men I'd watched on television. It's different somehow being thumped by a star and thumping him back.

This was the start of a toughening process that was to take Bath further and further up the rugby ladder. Not only were they extremely talented but they played a very physical game and every side seemed to contain a Welsh hit man. He wasn't picked only for his ability to play rugby but because when the chips were down he could throw a good right hook. If I had a quid for every stitch I picked up from one of those boyos, I'd have enough for an exceptionally good night out somewhere in the West End.

It wasn't unusual in the scrum for someone from the second row to aim one up into the hooker's face. It was so commonplace the referees didn't even bother to look for it. I learned very quickly that I had to fight to survive, the more so since I lacked skill. Another intimidating tactic you don't see so much now was the way they would try to bend you in

two in the scrum, pushing you down in a way that is none too good for the back. I may have the body of a thirty-year-old but I have the back of an octogenarian.

The games we played against the Welsh clubs began as ritual defeats but, little by little, being attacked the way we were, moulded us into a team. The fire of conflict forged us into a hard edged weapon and gradually we began to realise that the other English teams were becoming an afternoon's relaxation. And, more to the point, we were winning.

We were also training harder than ever. I doubt if the fans know what it is like to finish a hard day's work and then spend two hours of hard slog in icy mud. Warm summer and autumn evenings make training a pleasant prelude to the detailed testing of the local ale. But when it is icy rain, three nights a week of training before a match can get to feel like hard work.

It may have been hard work but it was beginning to pay off. We were starting to win on a consistent basis and, for the first time in my life, I was a true member of a team. I really

belonged. Being a member of a team like Bath to me means even more than playing for England - all the team know you well and most of the spectators know you well enough to know what beer to stand up. It is a huge and very friendly family and you are playing with, and for, friends all the way. That is a feeling I do not believe you could get from any game other than rugby.

Playing for England is the pinnacle of success, but it only happens for a few matches a year, whereas with your club you are training and playing together for up to nine months in twelve. Inevitably this builds up bonds between the members of club sides which perhaps cannot be attained at national level.

TRAINING IN THE RAIN
CAN BE A TERRIBLE STRAIN!

"Do what I do, charge it to Nigel Melville's room".

Mr T going to a fancy dress party as Gareth Chilcott.

Ann sitting on Father Christmas' knee at the mini rugby Christmas party.

Not more fancy dress, this was me acting as an usher, (doorman) at David Trick's wedding.

This year's body beautiful contestants, who did not make the final stages.

One of the few occasions that my sweatband had been used to keep sweat out of my eyes.

Photo: All-Sport Photograph

Gary Pearce, Brian Moore, and Gareth Chilcott, preparing for a scrum, Gary Rees and Dean Richards look on.

Photo: All-Sport Photographic Ltd

ENGLAND 11 FRANCE 0

4th March, 1989

Back Row (left to right): O E Doyle (I.R.F.U.)   S R Hilditch (I.R.F.U.)   S M Bates (Wasps)   G S Pearce (Northampton)   M D Bailey (Wasps)   P A G Rendall (Wasps)   W A Dooley (Preston Grasshoppers)   D Richards (Leicester)

D J Ackford (Quins)   M C Teague (Gloucester)   G J Chilcott (Bath)   C R Andrew (Wasps)   G W Rees (Nottingham)   S J Barnes (Bath)   J Olver (Quins)   B W Stirling (I.R.F.U.)

Front Row (left to right): C Oti (Wasps)   C D Morris (Liverpool St. Helens)   S J Halliday (Bath)   R Underwood (Leicester/RAF)   W D C Carling, Captain (Quins)   B C Moore (Nottingham)   J M Webb (Bristol)   R A Robinson (Bath)

Scorers: Tries—Carling, Robinson
Penalty—Andrew

BLUE BLACK AND WHITE RULES

BATH has in recent years enjoyed considerable success and it always hurts me when I hear commentators say "they recruit international players." This is such rubbish. We are not talking about football where you can buy talent.

There are 13 internationals in the Bath side at the moment but only two had caps when they joined, the others earned that distinction while playing with us. It is true to say that someone at Bath has had an eye for talent and has invited the right people to play with the side and nurtured them well. The only two capped players to join us were Stuart Barnes who came as an especially welcome chap after missing a vital penalty against us when we beat Bristol in a local derby cup final and Tony Swift from Swansea. Everyone else refined his game with the side and went on to earn a cap.

When I joined them in the seventies we had some pretty good seasons. We were a good team. But we never seemed to earn any silverware for the trophy cupboard. In fact, to my knowledge, in those days we didn't even have a trophy cupboard, it was certainly well hidden if we did. Having cut our teeth on some real tough rugby in the Welsh Valleys, we then became a lean and hungry side. When you are down, there is only one way - up. In 1984 the moment for up came when we won the cup for the first time.

Six years out of seven we took the trophy and 1987/8 when we lost, sharpened us in a way that turned us back into a hungry mob lusting after a display of silver - or is it plate? Many people outside the club felt we might go the same way as Leicester had done a few years earlier but that defeat merely spurred us on to greater efforts. Without wishing to sound conceited, the cup final day over the previous four years had become our day. Players and supporters in Bath had booked tickets and coaches for the Final a year ahead assuming confidently we would make it to Twickenham and win. Bearing this in mind the defeat was a major blow to players and supporters alike. It could not be allowed to happen again and, although at the time I would not have thought it possible, we trained even harder the following season. At the time of going to press, we have not lost the cup since.

One of the first things to be established once we had won at Twickenham was the traditional celebration which is now followed as if it were holy writ. On the way home the coach pauses for a swift gallon apiece of Guinness and port, which gives the forwards extra iron in their bodies.

We then return to the club house where, not to disappoint the supporters, we drink all night with them. Then on to Coach Jack Rowell's house for a champagne breakfast which seems to last until the pubs open at noon and it is time to go to the White Hart at Ford. A liquid lunch there and it is the moment to try and get onto an open topped bus with the mayor of Bath and enjoy the, by now rather unpleasantly loud, cheers of jubilant Bathonians in the streets of the Georgian city. Naturally we wind up this modest celebration with a curry.

I find it hard to say which of the many matches I have played was the most exciting, but I am certain of one thing, those cup finals where you are close to winning, helped by men you have worked and trained with for years, come out as some of the best moments of my career.

That first cup win in 1984 brought one great change to our lives. Where Bath used to have the odd brief tour in Southern France or perhaps Germany, we were now no longer afraid to go to the committee and ask for the cash to go somewhere a bit more exciting. They could hardly say no to you when you had just taken the sport's top trophy, watched by 50,000 people, could they?

The best benefit of the game is touring. It is an amateur game and long may it remain that way - but there are fringe benefits – being away from home for up to three months, with no need to dig your hand in your pocket for anything more than a postcard to send home, is the best.

Being with 25 friends and sharing the experience of other countries, other cultures and other liquor has a great deal going for it. Coming home after a long tour, to a land where there is no room service, no swimming pool outside the window, and you do not choose supper off a menu, can be a cultural shock. Add to that a mortgage and an employer who has thoughtfully ensured a busy in-tray on day one back, and you may understand why I would like life to be one long tour.

One of our earlier tours was to San Francisco which is the world capital of homosexuality and left quite a few of the players with a certain amount of cultural shock. We were never quite sure what we might be chatting to in a bar and we were certainly unused to such an open gay culture. But still, each to his own!

Florida on the other hand was much more up our street. I have never seen so many beautiful, tanned blondes in my life. Thanks to the heat they didn't seem to overdress much either and they made a welcome change, for me personally, from Frisco faggots. But I can't speak for all the boys. Even the trip to get there was quite exciting.

... AVOID STRANGERS WHO WANT TO KNOW WHAT YOU GET UP TO WHEN YOU SCRUM DOWN!

TOUR ITINERARY San Francisco

Thanks to a spot of industrial inaction by the air traffic controllers our party was split on to two flights from Gatwick, the one containing the committee and the well behaved players got away to Miami.

But the other containing yours truly and five other members of the front row found itself stuck without a plane. We were forced to spend seven hours in the bar of the departure lounge before being wheeled onto an aeroplane and served complimentary drinks to make up for the delay. The result of this was that I wasn't quite sure whether I was Atilla the Hun or Winnie the Pooh by the time I was helped off the plane and steered in the direction of customs.

No sweat as the Americans say. I knew we were staying at the Holiday Inn so it was no problem to stay in our tight group and ask the first taxi driver we met to conduct us to the Holiday Inn. We were not prepared for his reply:

"Which one bud? We got 23 here in Miami." There was only one thing to be done. We took refuge in the arrivals bar at Miami until four or five hours later somebody came to rescue us. That was a most enjoyable tour. The rugby was quite undemanding so that you could really enjoy the social life that makes the tour. And enjoy it we did.

The last stop was the best. This was in the deep southern town of Tallahassee which has the little known distinction of being one of the few places in the USA where the women outnumber the men by a considerable number. The University is the national centre for a great many courses such as domestic science and there are four girls to every guy. Not surprisingly a good many of the players left their hearts in Tallahassee.

The hub of the town was a club, called Bullwinkles, with a disco on the top floor, live music on the next one down and a lively bar on the ground floor complete with huge grounds in which to soak up the sun. Thanks to the ratio of the sexes one never lacked for a dancing partner, and that bar did better business while we were in town than it had for years.

Every tour has its own unique tour drink and this one was rum coolers – Bacardi with orange and lemonade. It sounds a pretty civilised drink for a rugby party, does it not? The only thing was we drank it by the pitcherful rather than the glass. If Florida was one of the tours that is memorable for some light games and fun social life, Canada was a more stern affair.

The rugby was much harder. The Canadians play a really physical game and this was made all the worse by our new captain, Roger Spurrell, who was a great believer in pre-season fitness and had a nasty habit of stopping the coach at the foot of a Rocky Mountain and getting us to run up it. This did not agree with my system very much and was actually quite dangerous.

It was in Fraser Valley in the Rockies, a place noted for scenery and nothing else that we had the hardest game of the tour. They didn't have a rugby team of their own so they recruited 15 lumberjacks, each six feet four tall and at least a yard wide who had spent months in the forest without a glimpse of a woman or any other home comfort. Their only recreation being to toss tree trunks lightly about and perhaps

bite the head off some furry little creature in the backwoods. These frustrated animals were let loose to work out their aggression on us. On rugby form the result should have been 60 to nil in our favour. The reality was the dirtiest game I have ever seen in my life which was abandoned by the ref with 20 minutes left to play, prior to the abrupt end of the game each lumberjack had fulfilled his ambition of belting a pom.

An illustration of this is poor old Nick Maslen who had spent sixty minutes in mortal combat with his opposite number at the back of the lineout, actually sixty minutes in mid air might be a more accurate description, as this particular opponent happened to be the Panamanian national 85kg wrestling champion.

That was one match I was really happy to view from the touchline rather than take part in, especially as the score was six nil against us when the referee stopped the fight.

The drink on that trip was as tough as the tour. We called it a B52 in memory of the American bombers that had been calling on Hannoi. Basically it was an unsophisticated little cocktail that required a shot of everything on the top shelf in a very large glass.

I have said that what spurred Bath to victory in the first place was hunger. Hunger for success. One thing that has kept us at the top is the desire to hold onto our newly discovered lifestyle. As a successful team we could persuade the committee to fund tours where we stayed in decent hotels and not on garage floors. We could visit exotic parts of the world and our hosts would really look after us.

The more we travelled together the closer we became as a unit and, naturally, a close team plays well together. One day we shall be knocked off our pedestal, that is inevitable but it will probably get us back again, fighting even harder than ever. I think Bath will be a top club for many a year yet and, as its oldest playing member, I plead the wisdom of age in this regard. But don't call me old to my face - I'm not that old yet.

PLAYING FOR ENGLAND

MY first cap for England ought to have been a red letter day in my life but instead it remains in my memory with a slightly nightmarish quality. Both the rugby and the subsequent social event were an unqualified disaster.

I got my chance to play for my country after Southwestern Counties had put up a heck of a fight against the Australian tourists and ending up with a twelve all draw that should have been a win for us. There was plenty of warning of the debacle that was the 1984 massacre of England by the Australians. The Aussies were a tough side that was cock-a-hoop having won the grand slam and who had been playing together for quite some time. We were an oddly assorted bunch of players, some like myself, young and green, with a trainer who must have had an Australian grandmother or some similar reason for wanting the tourists to win.

When someone compiles an Olympic style contest of all-time bad sports trainers I am backing Dick Greenwood to be on the rostrum. He was a fitness man but not a technician. We were not a totally unfit side but our only hope of making a good showing against the Aussies was to play a good tactical game. In the few days we had together before the match he sent us on runs. We might have had a match plan but I was unaware of it and we didn't know one another's style of play nearly well enough.

Thanks to television, we knew more about the play of the

other side than our own. On the morning of the match we were taken for a walk along the banks of the Thames and it was on this walk that I received my match instructions. England's rugby supremo put his hand on my shoulder and gave me the advice I was waiting for. He said intently: "England expects."

It may be my lack of education, pre-match nerves or just inexperience of playing for England, but that failed to totally explain the tactics I had to put into practice for 80 minutes, facing some of the toughest sons of convicts us Poms have had to contend with in many a long year. All these years and hundreds of matches later, I am forced to the view that this advice is something you try to avoid stepping in when crossing a field of cattle.

As surely as night follows day, the training presaged a match that was a total farce. After ten minutes of play hooker Steve Mills had to go off with a ricked neck. His replacement Steve Brain found himself locked in the stand and unable to reach the field, so, for ten minutes, I hooked until someone helped him to escape. Both of us were in the position of throwing in the lineouts to 19-year-old Nigel Redman with no idea of the jumper's signals. It is a little known fact that the first time Steve Brain and Nigel Redman met each other was that day on the pitch at Twickenham.

We had not done lineout practice in our lack of match preparation and so the Australians had an even chance when we were throwing in and a near certainty when they were throwing in to Steve Cutler who, at that time, was rated the number one lineout jumper in the world. I can laugh at it now but the frustration I felt at our total incompetence on the sacred turf of Twickenham, simply because our training time had been frittered away, boiled over.

As a result of a certain amount of needle between myself and their scrum half Nick Farr-Jones, I hauled off and punched him in the ear at the edge of a maul. Everyone in the stands saw it, 50 million television viewers saw it, every man jack of the England committee saw it, the referee had his eye on the ball and did not.

26

With that one punch I earned the popularity of a bacon butty at a bar mitzvah and one second of loss of control was to put me in the wilderness, as far as England was concerned, for the next eighteen months. The match continued in a way that I would prefer to forget and ended with the Australians winning 19   nil, they deserved their victory.

After a bad game there is always the consolation of drowning one's sorrows and perhaps redeeming the shining hour with the odd merry prank. The post match shindig was a dinner and ball at the London Hilton. It would have been nice for the players to have been able to get together and share their misery, but the RFU in its infinite wisdom had invited hundreds of well stuffed shirts, and a player was put on the table of each.

After the dinner the band of the Welsh Guards struck up with "In an English Country Garden" and couples began waltzing or foxtrotting, I can't tell the difference, while I stood morosely at the bar, staring into the glass of fizzy beer in my hand, wondering what the hell had happened to the rest of the team. Later I was to discover the secret of enjoying these RFU old boy binges, but the first one was as jolly an affair as a picnic in a catafalque. I've been to jollier cremations. I came back to the west country firmly convinced that if that was national rugby I'd sooner stick to Bath.

Despite the fact that I hadn't enjoyed a second of my debut for England, I was thrilled beyond measure when I got my second chance. This would prove that I wasn't a one cap wonder. Things were different this time. The coach was Martin Green and we went on the field as a team in a home international in which we defeated the Ireland team 25 - 20, a score which sounds closer than it really was for we were on top throughout the game.

This time I didn't get to play lemon at the dance either. I found out what the lads got up to while the gentry were trotting their foxes. Balls to the ball and off upstairs to the roofgarden bar on the 29th floor, where the aim and object of the exercise is to get as many drinks onto someone else's room tab as is humanly possible. On this occasion I was with

five others, all suffering a certain post match thirst and we managed to get £2,000 worth of drinks put on Nigel Melville's room bill.

The RFU used to pick up the cost of players' drinks and there was some sort of enquiry into how one man had drunk quite so much, until they noticed six rooms with no drinks on them at all. With cocktails at about four and a half quid apiece, it did not take long to add a couple of grand to poor Nigel's bill but it was still quite an achievement among six.

This was the second of a number of appearances for England and each time I was selected I was in competition with two other really good players - Geoff Probyn - you've got to be able to cheat as well as he can to survive against him, although he's a gentleman off the field and The Judge, Paul Rendall. Paul's nickname comes from the fact that when we are on tour he is in charge of justice. He judges the sinners and hands down some pretty tough sentences.

On an Australian tour, John Bentley had stepped out of line and was sentenced to be tied to a tree for the duration of

our super all night barbecue and to sing a silly song every five minutes throughout the night. Another wretched offender was Richard Hill, one of the smaller players on the tour, whose condign sentence was to consume the same quantities of food AND drink as I did for a full 24 hour period. After the first six or so the poor soul was comotose for the duration of his sentence.

After that terrible first appearance farce, I started to really enjoy playing for England and we did train together properly. The way it tends to go is that we get together during the three or four weekends before a major international and then on the Wednesday before the game itself we practice scrummaging, on the Thursday lineouts, rucking, and the formation of a team plan. Friday's training is really showmanship. We put on a bit of a display for the press and television. It's more for the benefit of the Nigel Starmer-Smiths of this world than serious training.

On the Friday night there's a visit to the theatre or a cinema and then to bed with a sleeping pill, because no matter how

many matches you have played you still suffer the most terrible nerves before a big game. Top actors will admit they get stage fright after 40 years in the business and rugby players are no different. For the three weeks or so from the moment when you know you have been selected there's a build-up of tension.

On the day, breakfast of your choice, then it's a police escort for the coach to the ground - are they trying to make sure we gladiators don't escape? The match itself flashes by and then you sit for half an hour or an hour in a daze trying to unwind and accept that it's all over. Thank God it's all over. A gallon or two of beer and then it's up early on Sunday morning to get the papers to find out how well we really did.

Match pressure is a very real thing. You spend the weeks from selection brooding on your opposite number and this may be one of the reasons there is a certain amount of violence on the field, with players having psyched themselves up to hate the guy before they have even met him.

One of the secrets of the current success of the England

team is its stability. I have been with it now for five years and we all know one another, get along together and play as a team. It was a completely different story in the early eighties when they were forever picking different players and there was no rapport within the team.

Since about 1986 they have got it right. To play well together you must know your team mate as a person and respect him as a man. The selectors now seem to appreciate that and have been picking some very strong sides. Like all British sports governing bodies the RFU is run by committees of oldish chaps who take two years to decide what colour to paint the door of the outside toilet.

The sport is run for the benefit of committees who are more concerned with where their next gin and tonic is coming from than the benefit of the players who are the game. When I retire, I may find myself on one of these committees and I hope I can kick some life into it. What the governing fossils fail to appreciate is that the game is changing every two years

and you don't have to be out of playing for more than a very few years to be out of touch with the game.

Once I have finished playing, the best way I can repay the sport that has given me so much is to find some way of slimming down the great committees. Something a little short of Hitler's Final Solution, but not much short, and of getting some young blood into running the game. Maybe that's what was meant by our charabanc coach with his "England Expects" prophesy.

One of my better bits of handling. Ann and myself on our wedding day.

Two of Donal's Doughnuts preparing for a pint of Guinness.

Photo: All-Sport Photographic

Taking a breather and trying to repair a dislocated bootlace at the same time.

Photo: Mihai Oroveanu

1989

I. C. Evans, C. M. Chalmers, P. W. Dods, G. J. Chilcott, R. A. Robinson, M. R. Hall, J. Jeffrey, D. B. White, J. C. Guscott, S. J. Smith, R. Andrew,

Dr. L. B. C. Gilfeather, G. Armstrong, A. Clement, D. Young, M. C. Teague, P. J. Ackford, W. A. Dooley, R. L. Norster, S. Hastings, M. Griffiths, B. J. Mullin, A. G. Hastings, K. Murphy, MCSP, Dip. PE.
(Hon. Doctor) (Hon. Physiotherapist)

B. C. Moore, R. Underwood, D. M. B. Sole, R. M. Uttley, D. G. Lenihan, D. C. T. Rowlands OBE, F. Calder, I. R. McGeechan, D. Richards, R. N. Jones, J. A. Devereux.
(Hon. Asst. Coach) (Hon. Manager) (Captain) (Hon. Asst Manager) (Coach)

Photo: Allsport Photographic Plc

If you think you can do better, get in the front row and prove it.

Giving Richard Hill as much protection as possible.

Filling in for Richard Hill when he is not available:

Helping Brian Moore to get dressed after an England training session.

THE BRITISH LIONS

FEW would dispute that the highest achievement in the career of any rugby player has to be taking part in a British Lions tour. This isn't necessarily because that is the best rugby you will ever encounter but it is more a measure of the scarcity value like truffles and caviar - there's not a lot about so it is more valuable.

The Lions only go on tour every three to six years so there are few players who have done more than one tour - it really is a once in a playing lifetime chance.

Like the girl with a curl, the Lions are either very good or very bad. Because the side are drawn from four or five nations, depending on how you view that island to the left of England on the map, you either end up with a fragmented side with the various groups polarised and not playing as a team or a completely united distillation of all that's best in rugby from England, Scotland, Wales, Ireland North and South.

They are either a success or a disaster and it was my luck to join them for a series of tests when there was no little cliques masquerading as a team but they got us all together to really play as a unit. The management, Clive Rowlands, Ian McGeechan and Roger Uttley had the right idea from day one. We were all given room mates from a different country and, after the afternoon familiarisation training, were given the order to go out on the town and get PISSED.

33

We obeyed our instructors with the blind obedience of religious converts. Within 24 hours and a similar number of pints we all knew one another very well indeed and the making of a team was there. The schedule was an intensive tour of Australia. I was very lucky indeed to even be on the tour having pulled a calf muscle playing for England in Rumania a fortnight earlier that gave me a fitness problem for the entire tour.

I am eternally grateful to our physiotherapist Kevin Murphy who worked on that calf muscle every day for the two and a half months of the tour. The poor soul is probably haunted by the sight of that leg to this day. Thanks to him I got to play some rugby but I am not certain I was the most cooperative of patients since resting up has never been one of my favourite activities.

What made the tour was a mixture of youth and experience. There were older players glad to share their wisdom and experience with the up and coming youngsters who were equally glad to learn from them. Finlay Calder was a superb skipper who led by example on and off the field. From day one he set up a series of committees, entertainment, accommodation and the like so that every player had a role of some importance off the field as well as on it.

Naturally I was on the entertainment committee. After a hard morning's training we organised some sort of relaxing activity, sailing, surfing, sight-seeing or even just videos to watch in the privacy of your hotel room, another form of sight seeing! This was fully supported by Ian McGeechan who realised that after each arduous day's training the need to relax is paramount for a successful tour.

After five days training and a match in Perth against Western Australia, which we won comfortably, our first real challenge came against a strong Australia B team in six inches of mud in Melbourne. We just scraped a victory with Dean Richards playing out of his socks and any illusion we might have had about an easy tour was shattered.

Our first test match in Sydney was lost. The Australians had the rub of the green. We allowed them to dictate the style of play and we followed it so we were well trounced. The tour was now at the crossroads, one test down and two to go. The telling game was the next against ACT, a side that had a habit of smashing touring sides and was notably aggressive. By half time we were behind but, after a half time pep talk as good as Mark Antony's oration over the body of Caesar, we went out again and went to victory. Robinson and Jeffrey's play is best described as inspired. They flew round the field and crashed through all opposition.

On a major tour there are two teams, a Wednesday and a Saturday side, the latter being the potential test team. On this particular tour the Wednesday team was nicknamed Donal's Doughnuts, the reason being we were superbly led by that great character and rugby player Donal Lenihan. Thanks to his inspired leadership this was not just a tour of the rugby venues of Australia but he also led his doughnuts into every single Irish Guinness drinking bar in the Southern Hemisphere. I treasure his remark at three in the morning after an aperitif of 15 pints of draught Guinness "The night

PITCH

FEVER PITCH

LIONS DRESSING ROOM

is but a pup". And he went on to sup another five or so before retiring safe in the knowledge that all his doughnuts were tucked up well before him.

With the victory against ACT thus retaining an undefeated midweek record, confidence was high for the second test at at Ballymore, Brisbane, which we had to win to have any chance of winning the series. After a very physical match and a bit of special magic from Jerry Guscott, victory was ours and the stage was set for the final test match at Sydney. This was one of the most thrilling games I have ever witnessed and a very close fought thing. The game hinged on a mistake made by David Campese who may be one of the world's most exciting wingers but he does make the odd mistake. On this occasion it fell to Billy Whizz, Iaeun Evans, to drop on the ball and score after Campese had lost possession behind his own line. We went on to win the test series two to one, a great achievement after being down and out after our first test defeat.

Mike Teague was voted man of the series and he certainly earned that title. I had played against him on many occasions and he was always a good and skilful player but on that tour he was at his peak of fitness and seemed to be everywhere on the field at once.

My saddest recollection of the Australians is that they like to hand it out but don't like it back. The papers were full of what hard men the Aussie teams were. Australians can outfight, outdrink and outwomanise any man in the world and they don't like it very much when someone proves they are wrong. We gave them some of their own medicine and it was not a case of whingeing poms but whingeing Aussies. For me this had a rather sad outcome.

On a previous England tour down under I found one of my opposite numbers was a gentleman called Peter Kay from New South Wales who was billed by the papers as the hard man of Australian rugby. He was a big guy and was a bouncer in night clubs in a very unsavoury part of the world where he was probably kept pretty busy.

During our match where I was playing tight head and he

was loose, we traded a few insults and a couple of blows but honours were pretty even and I was quite looking forward to buying him a drink in the bar and finding out what made him tick when, at the handshake ceremony at the end of the game, with television cameras on us, instead of shaking hands, he let fly a haymaker that just caught the top of my head.

Not surprisingly, I retaliated and put him on the floor before we were dragged apart. Despite the fact that I was defending myself against an attack at a time when hostilities were over, certain segments of the gutter press could not resist branding me as Chilcott the Animal or the Thug. Anyone who saw the incident on television will be in no doubt as to what really happened but what really saddened me was the thought that my wife, reading the tripe that appeared in some of the tabloids, might have got quite the wrong impression about what was happening all those thousands of miles away.

It says a lot for the philosophy of the two managements. Despite the fact that Peter Kay was seen by one and all to start that brawl, their selectors chose him for the next test and ours protected my reputation by keeping me with the side but avoided confrontation by not selecting me for that match. I missed a game thanks to that incident but it is interesting to see the difference between the two attitudes. The Aussies were full of gungho and fight until they got it back when we were branded by their press, players, supporters and all as a bunch of animals.

I have said that playing for the Lions is something that usually only happens once in a Rugby career, this may be at risk soon as World Cup rugby takes over. There is a danger that Lions tours may have to be cut down and, to a certain extent, commercial sponsorship may be the driving factor behind this change.

Rugby is a sport growing in popularity at the same time that football, mainly thanks to the thugs, is in retreat. More companies want to be associated with what is a family sport. You can take your wife and children in perfect safety to a rugby match, certain in the knowledge that the worst possible thing that could happen to them is hearing someone yell a rude word. There's plenty of the drinking that is blamed for soccer violence but you do not get it at rugby matches.

Thus firms want their products associated with this more wholesome product and, because that's the way commerce operates, are looking for a more obviously structured international sport. The sequence of a world cup makes more sense to them than the Lions roaming the world in search of a challenge and some fun. It would be a shame if their efforts to support what they see as a good, clean, wholesome sport changed it to the extent that we made the same mistake as association football.

ROAMIN' RUGBY CLUB

ENGLAND TOURS

PLAYING for England on tour is a great honour but it has its good sides and its bad ones. The greatest plus of all is that while, with club rugby, you may find yourself billeted with someone who expects you to be in bed and asleep by ten, you travel first class and stay in the best hotels touring with the national side.

On the minus side England only tours against the major rugby playing countries, notably Australia and New Zealand, while an inventive fixtures chap can get you to some really exotic places at club level. There is also the question of coming down from cloud nine. As an England player you are kitted out with blazer, grey flannels, shirts, socks, ties, shoes, training kit - the lot. Meals are available night and day in the good hotels where one stays and, despite the training, a good many players have problems with their weight on tour.

Coming home to the reality of the mortgage, a lawn

needing cutting and a pile of unpaid bills is a cultural shock, to say nothing of the basic problem of having to make a cup of coffee for yourself rather than yell for a waiter.

If you want to go out to a club or any other social activity, the hosts always have a liaison officer and you just tell him what you want and he rings the club and warns them, the England team is coming to visit you and drinks are always on the house.

While this book is not a kiss and tell but a ruck and remember best seller, I can retell the perfectly true story of an England player whom we had best call Fred, since that is nothing like his real name, who returned home to his loving wife from nearly three months on tour and instinctively got out of the marital bed at about two in the morning thinking he had to get back to the team hotel.

As his true position dawned on him and he began to realise where he actually was, a sleepy voice from under the duvet said: "It's alright, you don't have to go - Fred's on tour."

Of the tours I have done with England, probably the one I liked least was the World Cup, because we were stuck in the same hotel in Sydney for a month. No disrespect to Sydney, but we had seen most of what Sydney had to offer after the first week and were hankering for the variety that touring brings long before the game started. Our training routine was not a help. We did not start until ten which meant that it was not until after lunch that we were free to behave like tourists.

We did quite well in our early matches until we came up against the old enemy, Wales in Brisbane, we froze and we played our very worst game. It was atrocious and we came home the next day, tails between our legs.

The following year brings back one of my happiest and yet most terrifying moments, playing against Fiji. We were the only white men surrounded by a crowd of 30,000 very tall, very black islanders. When the Fijians had the ball the roars were so deafening, you couldn't hear another player shouting from a yard away and, when we had possession, there was a quiet, an ominous quiet that suggested the calm before a

storm. We were playing before their new president, just after a coup and he was an ex-rugby player himself.

It was in Fiji that David Egerton must have earned a spot in the Guinness Book of Records for a cap for the least time spent on a rugby pitch. In the dying seconds of the match one of their players was sent off for smashing Gary Rees' nose while Gary himself had to retire as floods of blood stopped play. His substitute was David who was still checking the laces on his boots, having run onto the field when the final whistle blew. We reckon he got a cap for five seconds on the field and didn't even have to clean his kit afterwards. In fact David Egerton is the only man I can think of who, in this situation, had the nerve to walk up to his opposite number and thank him for a good game.

The crowd may have been eerily frightening in some ways but I fell in love with Fiji and the Fijians. After the match there was a party the like of which could not have taken place in any other part of the world. It started with a drink made from a local boiled root called Karva. This little tipple tastes of aniseed and muddy water but it is some sort of drug and, apart from making you somewhat Brahms and Lizt, also has the same effect as a shot of Novocaine at the dentists. It makes the lips go numb with the effect that within minutes they had a couple of dozen British rugby players slobbering and drooling helplessly for their entertainment.

The party began at about 5.30 and concluded at about the same time the following morning as players, hosts and officials banded together in a mad, drunken frenzy to get everything and everyone packed in time for a six o'clock flight. The men of Fiji are huge, even the women run to six feet six but they are so friendly and hospitable they have a place in my heart forever.

That has to be in total contrast to Rumania which we visited the following year. Where on Fiji we were met with a drink and instructions to head for the beach, in Rumania it was men with guns and a feeling of repression everywhere. This was about five months before the popular uprising. The Rumanians themselves are colourful and happy people, the original gypsies but they were held down, repressed and almost afraid to speak to one another let alone a foreigner. I hope things are better for them now that they have shaken off the tyranny of their rulers. That was not the happiest tour we ever made.

America was an interesting place to tour. We would always beat an American side because, while they are big, fit and enthusiastic, they lack technique. In Britain rugby is a game played at a great many schools, while in the US football is the game and rugby is for guys who have not gone far enough in football. In other words they do not come to the game until they are in their twenties and, by then, what is bred into us they have to try to learn.

After most matches we would be asked to help with coaching sessions. They are very anxious to learn and I have no doubt that one day America will dominate the rugby world the way it dominates a great many other sports as soon as they start learning the game early enough in life and also get over their attitude problem.

I love America, it's a pity it's full of Americans. They have to be so macho. Everything has to be so much bigger and better than everywhere else and yet they are so naive. In a match at Boston one of their pack was a man mountain with muscles on his eyelids and biceps like the Rocky Mountains. In a lineout he warned us: "Hey man, I kick ass".

But the poor great dope knew nothing about rucking and, I am afraid got trampled into the mud and was off the field before the expiry of the twelfth minute. Probably the only "ass" he got to kick was his own. To his eternal credit, after the game he appeared, head swathed in bandages with an outstretched hand and a can of Budweiser and admitted "I guess I asked for that Buddy." For all that I find the boastful Yanks one of nature's haemorroids. I have to admire their dedicated pursuit of sporting excellence, and there is no doubt, that if rugby becomes more of a high school game there we shall have to watch our laurels because they will be back to beat us at our own game.

I just find people who find it necessary to drink beer out of a can and crush the tin in a single sweeping gesture, a trifle too anxious to prove their own masculinity to be really true. And there seem to be a great many such folk in the good old US of A. They still have a crusading spirit, the one that made them want to take on the communists in Vietnam with a penknife, and they try the same with visiting rugby teams. Technique will always triumph over skill-free enthusiasm.

I never did get to play in New Zealand, although those that did assure me that it always rains there and the scenery is a bit like the highlands of Scotland. They play a good hard game of Rugby but there's little else there. It has been suggested that this could be the armpit of the world but I wouldn't know, the nearest I got was Australia, a country of contrasts from the sun baked north to the damp south.

IN THE WILDERNESS

THROUGHOUT my career, I have had battles with authority. Committees, Disciplinary Committees and the rest. I probably have established something of an unenviable record by being sent off five times in first class matches.

There's a fine line between hard, aggressive rugby and foul play and I am the first to admit that in my early days in the sport, I was not too sure where that line was drawn. If for me there was ever a blinding light on the Road to Damascus it came in Boston, Massachusetts where we were having anything but a tea party.

We were up against Irish American IRA supporters and that was the most violent hour of my life and I was in some danger of really going over the top. Jack Rowell took me to one side and put it to me that I was in grave danger of letting myself, my family, my sport and my country down. He said I'd enjoy my rugby more if I concentrated on looking for the ball not the man. He was right and from then on I concentrated on fitness and technique and my play became more skilful and less violent.

One of the reasons that I have been in more trouble than most is that I don't exactly look like a pacifist and, if I do decide to cuff someone, I do not tend to do it in a sly way. I just haul off and clobber the guy and I am always caught. Those that live by the sword die by the sword. Unlike far too many of the hard men of rugby, I never run crying to

committees or the press if I am on the receiving end of a bit of rough treatment, but far too many do just that.

What I found strange was how many former rugby hard men get onto committees and then seem horrified at players doing what they had been doing only the season before. It seems poachers turned gamekeepers can be extra censorious. I suppose it is the zeal of the convert. Someone who has just given up smoking seems to kick up more of a fuss if anyone lights up near them than a lifetime non-smoker. And a heck of a lot of committee men behave like whores that have joined a nunnery, they put the old evil ways behind them - it's all overtime and no undertime any more.

My face doesn't fit in a great many areas. For example, I have played for England 14 times and have toured with the Lions but I have never been invited to play a match with the Barbarians. I am not their type of nice rugby player and, as far as I know, my old school tie is not one they would recognise - mainly because its principal function was as a garrotte.

46

The worst sending into the wilderness came in a Bristol match when I was sent off for stamping on Bob Hesford. Someone in authority had made the decision "let's make an example of Chilcott to let it be seen we are doing all we can to discourage violence on the pitch". I was banned from rugby for 13 months, the longest ban ever imposed and even on appeal they only lopped a month off.

Sometimes these exercises in showing how firm authority can have far reaching effects and all too often bear no relationship to natural justice. For example in an international against Wales at Cardiff Arms Park, there is no doubt that the first five minutes would best be described as a brawl. Wade Dooley was one of those involved and darned nearly lost his job as a policeman over the incident.

Yours truly, Graham Dawe and skipper Richard Hill were all banned. Poor Richard was banned even though he had no part in the fighting. Because he was the captain it was felt he should have had his lads under control. Quite how they thought he would prevent three 17 stone forwards throwing

a punch single handed I am not sure. Another aspect of the lack of justice is that four England players were carpeted. The Welsh team were treated as heroes. Does anyone honestly believe that the scrapping was one sided? If it takes two to tango, it certainly takes more than one to have a fight.

Of course one feels bitter about being punished for things that others are doing and getting away with scot free, but the judgement of the RFU does occasionally seem curiously blinkered. Players all over the world are paid. Only England really operates the true amateur status. If you think French rugby players are amateurs, look at the cars they use to drive to matches with advertisements on the sides then look at the England stiffs representing their country on £14 a day loss of earnings.

Would it really bring the fabric of the sport crumbling if players were allowed to be paid for an after dinner speech, an article for the press, opening a fete? I fervently believe that it is in the long term interest of the game that it remains an amateur sport for as long as possible. But you also have to accept that a top rugby player spends as much time training and playing as any footballer and that, when he has come to the end of his career, all he can say is "I travelled the world and I played rugby for England". That is hardly a qualification that fits onto the job application form boxes.

A good many of the senior people in the RFU either had degrees or family money when they were playing and so it was no great financial hardship. What do you do in your thirties or early forties when you cannot play any more and have not even earned enough money to get up the housing ladder, let alone the professional ladder. Employers who are prepared to give you three or four months off to go on tour are not as thick on the ground as they used to be. I would hate to see my sport spoiled by the money and stardom that has taken soccer from the community game it was to its present state. I am one of the lucky ones having managed to find a career that gave me the scope to play and yet progress. But I cannot ignore the fact that, were I a football player, I would be called a star. And I would not live in a terraced house in

Little John (Wade Dooley) and myself doing battle.

Andy Robinson, Gerry Guscott and me. Three Bath players representing the British Lions.

David Sole (ex Bath) and Dean Richards trying to figure out why he is in the photograph.

Giving Gary Rees and Gary Pearce some hints on front running. Rory Underwood is just behind Gary Pearce!

On the 'slippery' slope, but still happy, with life.

Donal Lenihan the victorious Wednesday side captain.

Donal's doughnuts at Base Camp.

Concentrating on keeping everything straight and on an even keel.

an unpretentious but friendly part of Bristol, I would have a mansion. Not that I would swap homely Eastville for Sneyd Park or Clifton, but there's a heck of a gulf between the rewards for the same amount of effort.

One of our players at Bath, Jerry Guscott, was reputedly offered a £300,000 golden hello to go and play Rugby League. To a man whose only income was on a building site, I do not know how he said no. We managed to get him a rather better job with British Gas and he's being a hero by not taking up the huge money he could earn by going to Wigan, or a similar northern club. Surely that is a remarkable sacrifice for a man to be asked to make.

Hypocrisy rears its ugly head when you look at the South African situation. I was invited to take part in the so called rebel tour of 1989 but, before I had a chance to weigh up the finances and morality of the situation, was offered a much more sound, long term business proposition in this country that would have made it impossible to go.

I got a letter from that little sports minister urging me not to accept the invitation. I presume diamond and gold bullion importers don't get too many letters asking them not to buy from South Africa. As far as I know all the uranium for our nuclear deterrent comes from there and there's no beef about improving our balance of payments by exporting to them. It is the sportsman who is being asked to carry the can. Business contacts are fine. Make money out of them but don't play games with them. If you really want to hurt anyone you aim for the wallet, you do not simply refuse to join in harmless recreation.

The RFU today is not too bad, but in my early days in the game it was ruled almost exclusively by port sodden, gout ridden old freeloaders who were totally out of contact with the game. They rather regarded the players as coarse fellows, whose duty was to provide them with an hour or so of outdoor entertainment between a copious lunch and a liver fattening dinner. Typical has to be the occasion when we got totally out of hand when playing against France in Paris. The team was based in a chateau type hotel in Versailles. On the

49

day of the match we were taken by coach into the centre of Paris with a police escort and roundly defeated by the French team.

There was a dinner after the match, following which the committee nomenclatura retired to the Hotel Concorde with free drinkies and snacks available all night. The team were sent a dozen miles out into the sticks to a hotel whose bar was shut and no amount of s'il vous plait was going to open it. We couldn't have afforded the prices in central Paris and here we were in a place that was as exciting as certain parts of Wales used to be on a Sunday.

We wanted a party, so we all went to our rooms and stripped down the mini bars, those tempting little fridges full of miniatures that cost un bras et une jambe and assembled in the corridors of floor three where we began one hell of a party. There was drinking and singing and we were getting back the camaraderie that had been damaged by the defeat of the afternoon, while drinking the lack of health of the committee with their exclusive party that shut out the very people who had made their trip possible.

Just how the fire extinguisher fight began I cannot recall but I know just how it ended, the whole of floor three was soaked from end to end. The foaming stuff was in the rooms, up the walls and all over the doors. The place looked like something from Beirut not Paris. I remember vividly one of the selectors, Derek Morgan, gibbering with rage holding up his dripping airline ticket and screaming at me: "Chilcott, you'll never wear a white shirt again." He was true to his word and I didn't get selected for England again until he was off the panel.

On the other hand, Mike Weston, who was our tour manager and was also chairman of the selectors took the view that it was only part, view that it was only part the committee's fault for booking us into an elegant morgue and dug into his own pocket to help us pay for the damage. We all chipped in and the Froggies got their third floor redecorated courtesy of the England rugby team. I cannot defend our action that night, which certainly pushed back the frontiers of hooliganism an inch or two, but I can say it came from a "them and us" attitude of the RFU.

Today things are better. In the old days, there was one token player on each table at the dinner after the match with nine committee men. Now the teams dine together and we also get on better with the men at the back of the sport. People like Geoff Cooke and Roger Uttley have done a great deal to repair management and shop floor relations in the sport of rugby. Not that we are unique. Tennis and football suffer from an acute, nigh terminal case of ancestor worship, with yesterday's men trying to dictate to young sportsmen. Has beens trying to hold back hopefuls seems to be a factor that badly afflicts most British sport.

The disciplinary hearings are something else. You are treated just like a schoolboy being summoned to the head's study. Called out of practice, you leave the field to cheers from the other lads and are made to sit outside the Coaches room for a suitably demeaning period, before being made to sit in front of the all powerful committee at a smaller desk and chair than theirs, while your knuckles are rapped in

suitable schoolboy form. Then it is back onto the field to applause from the others.

The whole thing is desperately childish, but it has to be said that on occasions our behaviour has been somewhat puerile, but two wrongs are not reputed to make a right. In the main we get up to more pranks on club tours and try to make the national side a slightly more dignified affair.

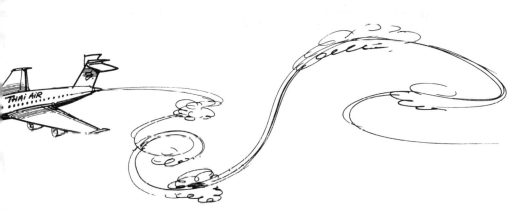

MIDDAY EXPRESS

AIR PIRACY is the offence for which I was arrested when on my way to Thailand, but it seems a rather grand way to describe the meeting of English and French rugby players in mid-air. I didn't want to pinch the man's plane, I simply wanted to knock the head off a Frenchman who had attacked a friend of mine. The tale began with flight 124 of Thai Air leaving Heathrow on schedule with, amongst its passengers, Chilcott G on his way to help coach the Thai national team, and old friend Martin Shepherd, who may have had training the Bangkok masseuses in mind. He was on holiday and only here for the beer.

Later, one of the air hostesses stated that we had drunk the aircraft dry before it reached the French coast. If this were true it must have carried woefully inadequate stocks, but then it was all free, and there is a limit to the generosity of any airline. We made a stop at Paris where we picked up a French rugby team from Agen, one of their better sides as it happens, and here the seeds of disaster were sewn.

One or two of their lads could speak English and we had a few beers together, which seemed wonderful for the first couple of hours, until that old Anglo-French rivalry began to make itself felt. The world knows the Brits play better rugby than the Frogs but no one has told the Frogs about it. Put it down to fear of flying, the beer in the terminal - what a lovely name for a place when you are in fear of your life - terminal - but we took them on at wine drinking. For Rosbifs to take on froggies at wine drinking, when the gallic onion sellers clean their teeth in the stuff, is insane and doomed to failure.

We upheld the honour of Britain for a creditable length of time and a great many glasses of plonk, before they began to sing the Marseillaise and we tried to drown it out with God Save the Queen, although we were having some trouble remembering either the tune or the words by this time. A certain pushing and shoving ensued, which was a pity because Martin, who was having enough difficulty maintaining a vertical position without outside hindrance, went flying down the aisle, hit his head on a seat and was out cold.

Knight in shining armour Gareth springs to the rescue and belts one of them. The blow was totally cushioned by the fact that I still had my plastic beaker in my hand and the only effect was to soak me in red wine. It was probably a combination of having not sliced the poor guy open and alcoholic idiocy, that I stood for a second or so giggling, before I remembered the object of the exercise was to avenge the fate of poor Martin. So I nodded in the guy's direction instead and that did the job.

I then proceeded to hit four more for six without receiving a single punch in return, which was a hell of a lot easier than it sounds because they were wearing seatbelts and not terribly mobile. The stewardess was obviously not used to the slightly eccentric way in which the international camaraderie of rugby manifests itself, for the poor frightened little soul locked herself in the flight deck and persuaded the

captain that the lives of all were at risk. He made an emergency landing at Karachi where uniformed guys with rifles poured onto the plane, bashed my groggy friend Martin on the head with a gun butt for crawling round the aisle and slapped the handcuffs on me.

We were marching across the tarmac in the blazing sun when another idiot idea came to me - make a run for it. Handcuffed, I ran as if I were making a break for the line. Those guys had real rifles. How I did not get my head blown off I shall never know. Of course there was nowhere to run and I found myself locked up for a couple of days in solitary, until they managed to get me on another flight to Bangkok, probably anxious to get rid of me They put me in an aircraft cabin full of tourists, with the final warning that if I ever set foot in Karachi again I would be shot.

In Bangkok without passport or luggage, I found myself a guest of the security forces once more, until somebody who spoke more English than the rest gradually appreciated that here was the long awaited coach for their rugby team.

The Thais do not play much rugby in schools, the main teams come from the Army, Navy and universities. Thanks to this they do not have too many cash problems and I was accommodated at the Hyatt Regency and chauffeured around like royalty. The main Bangkok pitches are at the Royal Sporting Club, a very upmarket and elegant affair with golf, tennis and racing as its other sports.

Such is my luck that they'd had a really severe monsoon that had flooded half the country, with the result that most of the military players were helping out on flood relief. The remainder were looking at where their pitches used to be before the rain washed them away. I was afraid they'd send me straight back but they were so charming and apologetic.

I was provided with an apartment overlooking the most heavenly beach, blue sea and sunsets, the like of which I have never seen in my life before. It was paradise marred only by the presence of between 30 and 40 bars within five minutes walk and a massage parlour next door. While I am not prepared to go into much detail about which won, the beach

or the beautiful Thai girls, I will say I was single and unattached at the time.

In thirteen weeks I did two rugby training sessions, both on the blackboard and I am far from certain what good they did. The interpreter may have spoken good English but he was having considerable difficulties with the Bristolian version of the language of the noble bard and most of my audience had a more than usually blank look for easterners.

UB40 to MD

WHEN I left school, I did not have any qualifications whatsoever and it is thanks to rugby that I am the managing director of a quite successful company and not behind bars. I spent my first year out of work with nothing more exciting to do than spray my name on the back of a bus shelter. Rugby gave me an interest in life and I started getting jobs that would allow me time to play. These were jobs you didn't mind losing.

I worked as a petrol pump attendant (remember them?) in a garage. One day an elderly lady in a huge Rover came with a flat tyre. Whether it was in anticipation of a fat tip or my natural desire to help older people I cannot say, but I rushed out with the big trolley jack, whizzed the car up and changed the wheel for her.

Being green in the matter of motor cars I did not know you should not put the jack under the sump. Apparently the car went two miles down the road before it over-heated. The bottom of the sump had cracked under the weight of the car and every last drop of oil drained out so that the engine seized. I was only paid £8.50 a week in those days so I could hardly buy the lady a new engine. The boss was very understanding and sorted her out. He didn't even sack me, although I think he did dock a few pounds from my pay for a week or two.

One fun job I had was as a lumberjack and quite a few of

the lads at Bath would come to me for a few days casual work to make some beer money. One was Charlie Ralston, an orthopaedic surgeon. He had been given a job in the Midlands where he was not due to start for several weeks and fancied a couple of days in the forest to make the price of a few pints. I think he thought it was going to be a soft option.

I picked him up at six in the morning and it was off to the woods - not a cafe or a pub in sight, a one and a half mile walk to the site through sleet, over frozen ground. The first job of the day was to drag out cut timber with the winch on the tractor. I left Charlie to start up the tractor and there was a plaintive howl - his hand had frozen to the metal of the machine. So that was the end of that day!

You have only to look at me to realise that I have the natural physique that makes me ideal for one job - debt collecting. I took it up partly in the hope of meeting ravishing young housewives in skimpy negligees who would offer payment in kind. We have all heard the tales of door to door salesmen. And debt collectors do much the same sort of round. In fact they are probably trying to get the money for the things the doorstep salesmen foisted on them the month before.

I certainly met a lot of housewives. Most wore curlers in their hair and tights under their sandals. It is amazing how the excuses were always the same. You would not believe how many husbands on a Taunton council estate were either working on a North Sea oil rig or had left their wives. Not that I could blame them for that. The ones who owed money were certainly not love's young dream.

The only person who ever offered me any violence was a Pakistani from Hayes, Middlesex, who threatened to throw me out of his shop. Since he only stood four feet tall including his turban, I thought he was rather brave but I stood my ground and we sorted it out amicably and I even got paid.

Bouncing is another ideal job for rugby players. I would do two or three nights a week at twenty pounds a night. It kept the wolf from the door. But I have to admit it is a mug's game. One day you are bound to meet someone bigger and

harder than yourself who will break a bottle over your head.

I could smell trouble. It always came from the same types - small guys, loud and full of lager. We used to call them Jack Russells - no disrespect to the current English wicket keeper. Sometimes we would look forward to a bit of action. Life was boring just standing by the door or on the corner of the bar. Some of the free-for-alls were a bit reminiscent of playing against the Welsh.

One tip I would give to anyone contemplating a career as a bouncer is walk to a fight or run away from one, not the other way around. I did it wrong one night, I ran to a fight and my leather shoes slipped on the stairs and down I came like a human avalanche. I flattened the two lads who were fighting - literally and damned nearly broke my back into the bargain.

Another job I had was laying pavements. I laid half the pavements in Keynsham, which is between Bristol and Bath, one long hot summer. The worst of that job was you were working right out on the street and could hardly take your

clothes off to keep cool. Ground work on a building site was another job to keep me in food and clothing.

The headache with playing our sport at a senior level is finding a job that can allow you two months off every year for touring. Usually you have to accept a non career job such as the ones I have described that you can leave to go on tour. It is alright for the chaps with Oxford or Cambridge degrees, they still stand a chance of getting a good job when they retire in their thirties but for chaps with no education this can be a problem.

I was lucky. A keen supporter of Bath, Malcolm Pearce, offered me a job in his firm, Johnsons Wholesale News, as a security man in 1987. Malcolm is a fanatic supporter of Somerset Cricket Club, Bath Races and Bath FC (RFU). He helps players at the club either by taking them on himself or getting them jobs with his friends. To rugby players he is an angel. I didn't stay in security for long. We set up a new division of the company called Chauffeurlink which provides an up-market car service. Probably the cheapest vehicle in the fleet is a BMW and we have more than one Rolls. We supply cars and drivers for everything from weddings to company functions. The greater part of our work is for large firms. It is amazing how it helps make a sale if you pick up the visiting buyer from the station or airport in the right kind of chauffeur driven limousine.

As managing director of Chauffeurlink, my tasks are pretty varied - from negotiating hirings with the transport manager of a multi-national to washing down a vehicle when there's no one else free to do it. I do a bit of driving when we are short handed and I can honestly say that no two days are the same - there's no danger of boredom.

I have tried to develop the business in different directions - one service we offer is half a day or a day's clay pigeon shooting. This can be used for client entertaining or rewarding staff. They go to the shooting grounds in something comfortable like a Renault Espace, which does service as a mini bus, have a bit of tuition, blast a few clays and a good lunch then home in comfort.

For me the worry of having to try to find a career that would make me enough money to service a mortgage after hanging up my boots, has been solved by Malcolm Pearce, and a bit of effort on my part.

VIEWS

RUGBY is an amateur sport and it should stay that way. I would hate to see my game corrupted by money in the way so many others have been. But that does not mean to say there should be no rewards for the top players. Why the top players and not everybody, I hear you mutter. It is fair to say that only the top football players make any real money out of their sport. There are hundreds of thousands who play every Saturday just for love of the game

There are still a few dinosaurs on the committee of the RFU who feel the game should be for the old school tie chaps with plums in their mouths and they lay down impossible rules for working class players. I don't feel anybody should be paid for playing rugby, but I do not see why on earth they should not be allowed to make a few pounds out of after dinner speaking, writing books, opening shops and that sort of thing.

I accept that this will mean the more charismatic players will do better than those whose personality does not suit. For better or worse I am instantly recognisable and I cannot go anywhere without people knowing who I am. Typical of the sort of thing which I think is wrong is when I was telephoned by an advertising agency to pose for a poster promoting low alcohol lager. I rang the club secretary to check if I could do it and Dudley Wood of the RFU said there was no way he could stop me, but was not happy about it, because with those thousands of posters by every roadside, people would never believe I wasn't paid for it. Eventually I agreed to do the job and was taken to a studio in London for the shot. The week before they took my picture, Ian Botham had been photographed in there to promote another commercial product and I can assure you his fee was not £500 to be given to charity. It was very considerably more.

In my case £500 went to the UPCC, Under-privileged Childrens' Charity. If rugby were not an amateur game I could easily have asked and got ten times that fee. Firms are quite keen to be associated with our sport because it is a family sport with a clean image and no crowd problems at all. It is also fair to say that, as always, Britain is the only one obeying the rules to the letter. Just as the Olympics consists of American professors of sport competing with Russian sporting colonels, there are plenty of people round the world who are paid to play rugby.

Underhand payments do go on and everyone knows that, even the RFU. I would like to see two reforms. One is the establishment of a trust fund into which a certain amount of money could be put for each match played, so that, when a player retires, he can draw out enough to sort out his mortgage. I am not talking of milking a poor sport. Twickenham is always full. If it were twice its size it would be full. Tickets for an international cost between £10 and £18 apiece and yet the chaps the 70,000 supporters have come to see never get a penny piece of that million pound take. Add to that sponsorship and advertising, the RFU takes a great deal of money, money which could be used for the benefit of the players.

When we are playing abroad we get £18 a day for loss of earnings and nothing at all if we are playing in this country. I cannot see any real objection to being allowed to open fetes or shops for a fee like every other sportsman does. I am not even going to be allowed to take any of the royalties from this book which is giving you little orgasms of pleasure at this very moment. The changes which I would like to see are not going to change the face of rugby as we know it, but just might make life easier for the players who are, after all, the game itself.

On the broader front, I'd like to see politicians stop using sport as a weapon. The boycotting of the Olympics by Americans upset at Russian actions, black countries who think people are too friendly with South Africa and all the rest of the tiresome nonsense simply degrades sport.

There's no shortage of South African produce in the shops and I don't see housewives consciously avoiding Cape oranges and yet, had I played a few games of rugby in South Africa, I would have been an outcast. What real rubbish. Contact at a sporting level is where we might be able to influence the thinking of young South Africans. But a guy who is haggling over the price of a container load of grapes is not going to influence the attitude of the merchant with whom he is dealing.

The reason sport is being used as a stick with which to beat South Africa is because the other African states cannot afford to stop doing business with them but cutting sporting contact

costs nothing. Perhaps we could stop buying South African coal and play cricket and rugby against them now that their teams are all multi-racial. We can afford to cut trade links if we feel it would be helpful. Although I have to admit that I have never thought that to stop talking, as a good way to resolve differences.

Free trade for sportsmen is my motto, although I am not quite so certain that applies to our football fans. If we sent them to South Africa, they'd probably boycott us.

LIFE AT THE TOP

LIFE as a sports celebrity has its compensations, you get to meet people and go to places that are denied to other folk, but at first it seemed a very strange world indeed for a lad from Bedminster. To begin with, I found it over-awing to have a lord sitting alongside me at dinner. I soon discovered that he was there because of his love of rugby and we had plenty to talk about after all.

I shall never forget my first really posh dinner, sitting on the top table. It was in a large cafe in the West End of London called the Savoy and, naturally, it was a black tie affair. I put on my dinner jacket, which had been my bouncer's uniform, and hoped that the invisible mend from where it had been ripped by a lager lout I was tossing lightly out of a nightclub, would not be discovered. The shirt collar refused to do up and I felt about as comfortable as a vegetarian at a butchers' convention.

A beer in the bar cost half a week's wages and everyone else seemed quite at home. Finally the dinner came and there in front of me was a complete cutlery set. Enough gleaming cutlery to perform major surgery. But no nurse to hand me the right scalpel for the first incision. Have you ever looked into the Snap-On Tool boxes they have in the bigger garages? That's what was parked on the table in front of me and I had no idea what spanner fitted what. Do you start from the left or the right?

Of course the answer is simple, you wait for someone else to make the first move and follow suit. The trouble is that, as guest of honour, they wait for you to start. There could have been an acute case of malnutrition that night had someone not tucked in, unaware that I had not started. I took my cue from him and away we went. The red wine helped me relax and, by the end of the evening, I was totally relaxed. Relaxed as a newt probably, but I had got through an ordeal successfully and mega formal dinners have been no problem ever since.

The one thing that always strikes me about the very ritzy dinners - what small portions they serve, there really isn't much to eat. I get invited to do after dinner speeches and to begin with they were the most nerve wracking experience of my career. I wouldn't taste the food. Not that it is necessarily purely nerves. At rugby dinners it is traditional to serve beef so thinly sliced that it is translucent with dilute gravy poured over it. This is served with sprouts that have been on the boil for a week before they are produced and the waitresses are trained to drop one of these in my lap every time. I cannot tell you rugby players are always regaled with this fare but I cannot remember a dinner where anything else was on the menu.

In the early days a petrified Cooch, who is afraid of no man but scared witless of public speaking, would stand up with quivering notes in a hand shaking so much that reading them was out of the question and, unable to make any sense of the notes, I'd start telling a few rugby stories and this usually went down pretty well. Today I've given up notes, I just have a card or two with a jotting of what stories I plan to tell.

My first experience came at Exeter University when I went down to address 250 very bright university students. I travelled with the Scottish prop David Sole and Roy Palmer which meant a few beers had been consumed before the dinner began. I had asked the people who had invited me to provide me with a script but they had done nothing. During the meal I ate nothing, I drank nothing, my mind was a blank.

Then to make matters worse, the 1st XV Captain got up and spoke for fifteen minutes - in rhyme. How on earth can you follow a chap who has been spouting verse for a quarter of an hour. The only verses I know would not really be suitable for an academic gathering. All I could do was get to my feet and tell a few impromptu rugby stories. They gave me a standing ovation. I do not know to this day if they were sorry for me or enjoyed the tales. But of one thing I am certain, I didn't enjoy that dinner.

My favourite dinners are with my first club the Old Reds. I enjoy sitting well away from the top table and being able to down a few beers and throw the bread around and generally act like a kid.

Pretty obviously you get introduced to a great many important people and not always with the results that were intended. I recall on tour in Canada we were filing into the dining room and being introduced to the High Commissioner and his wife in the doorway. I'd had a sniff of the barmaid's apron and to this day I cannot remember where I got it from, but I had a glass of red wine in my paw as I went to shake hands with Mrs Commissioner and it went all down her white ball gown. She was pretty good about it really and assured me that it would wash out and the dress wasn't quite new … the powers that be of rugby were less understanding and I got heavily fined for that piece of clumsiness.

Once after a game Steve Brain introduced me to an old friend of his, Jasper Carrot. The trouble is he did not actually make any introductions because he felt we were both well known faces. Yes I knew the face but couldn't place it. After a few halting exchanges of conversation I tried to pin down where I knew this guy from: "Have I ever played against you?" I enquired. I accept he hasn't the build to be a forward but he could have been a winger couldn't he?

I fared better when I met Princess Anne. She wanted to know why I wore a headband since it was obviously not to keep my hair out of my eyes - what hair? I explained that I was trying to avoid getting yet another cauliflower ear and that the Vaseline on my neck was to prevent skin burns from the fabric of the shirts. For once, I managed to get through a formal chat without using any four letter words or making a fool of myself in any way whatsoever.

Once you become recognised as a celebrity people recruit you to do daft things for charity. One I remember with slight horror to this day was a celebrity car race round Brands Hatch. We had practice the day before and a bit of tuition. With an empty track I was doing quite well and throwing the XR2 Turbo round quite nicely. When the day dawned stage fright took over. Packed grandstands turned my knees to jelly and that got reinforced when the car in front of me spun off demolishing all sorts of things at Druids.

From that moment I drove as if I was on my test. I don't think I got out of third and everything was lapping me. When I pulled in after all the rest, I discovered I'd done nine laps instead of ten. The supreme accolade came from one of the rude mechanics in the pits: "I've seen a dog walk faster round the course than that," he said flatteringly. The funny thing is I am normally quite a fast driver.

During the Telethon some child of unmarried parents decided that I should eat a couple of tons of Mexican enchilladas to help the children in need. Now I hate enchilladas. I cannot stand the things. I discovered the reason I had been lumbered with this distasteful task was my moustache. I would not have called that a Pancho Villa tache myself but there is no accounting for the strange minds of television folk. I don't think I dented the world enchillada gobbling record which is a pity because I have quite a big belly and had the fare been something rather more toothsome, might have set the odd Olympic guzzling record.

It is surprising what you will do for charity. I've done sponsored walks, runs, swims and lord knows what else besides, I've even sipped a low alcohol lager. And to set the record straight, I do not drink low alcohol beer. Unless I have to drive, give me the real thing every time. Once in Australia they got me dressed up as Oddjob, the psychopathic oriental who kept chopping people's heads off by throwing his bowler at them like a frisbee. This was in aid of some children's charity or other but for the next three months of the tour I was bombarded with frisbee beer mats and greeted with Ah Sos.

Probably the most embarrassing was when Dean Richards, Brian Moore and I got conned into helping publicise the renaming of the London Ballet Company, the Royal Ballet. We were dressed up in tutus for a photo call. Those pictures didn't just appear in the tabloids, even the Times and the Telegraph used them. The Dance of the Rugger Scrum Hairies was big in every paper in the country. We just wanted to hide and we had to play France the next day with them laughing up their sleeves about les poofs. There was only one thing we could do, we went out there and thrashed them. Part of the reason for that victory over the French was the need to retrieve a spot of shattered morale.

I say I have done a great many things for charity and have turned down few stunts in a good cause but I do draw the line at parachute jumps. I do not like heights and I have a horror of falling but someone once did get me up on a chute for the first and last time in my life during a Far Eastern tour.

People had been parascending all day and how I got conned into being the team guineapig I'll never fully understand. The Malaysian gentleman explained how it worked. You put on the parachute harness clipped on a line to the back of a speedboat and walked down the beach filling the chute, the line tugged you up in the air and all you had to do was admire the scenery. Sounds pretty straight forward would you not say?

In my case, being a mite heavier than the little oriental chaps who had been whisked away under the chute, it was proposed that I should run and give a little bunny hop when the line tightened to get myself airborne.

That was the moment when the boat pulled me off my feet and dragged me on my belly down the beach, at what seemed like a hundred miles an hour, before the chute lifted me up. The harness took a vice-like grip on what is normally protected from such assaults during a rugby match by a jock strap. For five minutes, that felt like five years, I was suspended by the tenderest part of my anatomy in sheer agony a hundred feet over a beach full of laughing people.

When I got down I was walking like John Wayne. I do not remember such an embarrassing and painful experience in my life. The insides of my thighs were raw, I felt as if I had ridden a carthorse bareback across the Arizona desert and, to make me feel better, my team mates were in hysterics. That I am still capable of reproduction is no thanks to the Malaysian parascending industry or my colleagues in sport.

Rugby has given me my fair share of embarrassing moments, but it has also brought me some wonderful moments of triumph, saved me from being an out of work drifter and ultimately brought me to a good and responsible job and a very happy marriage. I owe everything I have and everything I am to the world's greatest game - RUGBY.

And, at the start of the 1990-91 season, the furthest thing from my mind now is retiring, I am going to go on playing for as long as anyone will let me.

ACKNOWLEDGEMENTS

I cannot let this opportunity pass without thanking Malcolm Pearce, Chairman of Johnsons Central Holdings. Without Malcolm this book would never have been more than an idea rolling around in the back of my head. Without Malcolm I might still be drifting from job to job without a future. I would like to say that Malcolm had the faith to employ me within his security division three years ago and has subsequently given me the opportunity of running Chauffeur Link, one of his many business concerns.

Tony Ferrand also deserves special thanks for making himself available to fit in with my schedule and managing to make some sense of the many stories I have related to him.

Finally, my thanks to Colin Higgins, David Trick and all at the Press and PR Company, Bath. I never realised there was so much involved.

Gareth Chilcott
September 1990